Elegies

Of A Goddess

Written By

Mylia Tiye Mal Jaza

Dedicated to all, written with hopefulness and love.

Elegies Of A Goddess

Written By
Mylia Tiye Mal Jaza

Edited By
T. Shani Scott

Cover Art By
Sun Child Wind spirit

Elegies Of A Goddess

ISBN 10: 7755196712
ISBN 13: 9788693484543

Author
Mylia Tiye Mal Jaza
myliajaza.gqnu.net
mylia@bepublished.biz

Self-Publishing Associate

BePublished.Org
Dallas, TX
mari@bepublished.org

Mary M. Jefferson
P.O. Box 8324
Jackson, MS 39284

Second Edition

Printed in the United States of America.

Recycled paper encouraged.

TABLE OF CONTENTS

time
life

Since You Brought It Up

As if the unmarried reek toxic fumes and I beg to be prey
Marriage and when is mine is the topic of marred folks' tome
When will I have kids is the most popular question day after day
Despite the occasion that's how the conversations sway
I stumble into this circle that seems more like a maze
Pressured even by those whose marriage is on the decay
I guess misery loves company is truly an applicable cliché
Choosing not to shatter globes I verbally go the other way
Opting instead to have other truths as the only words I say
I'll try to reach only for kind and diplomatic lingo to spray
As I discuss the black-and-whites and address shades of gray
Starting with there are no plans to spew illegitimates from my bay
Why encourage another to rush into a child and spouse anyway
With most marriages becoming divorces why enlist in the display
I don't want repetition of episodes identified as problems today
I have no esteem hang-ups and let none do to me what he may
Decisions are conscious and are as varied as uses for mayonnaise
Time alone gives the soul the field on which it can freely graze
Good times don't always require others or a ticket to Paraguay
I can't vow to accept the bad for the promise of a daily lay
I lack no male affection and have no reason to beg any to stay
I am already joyfully whole and my life is in no disarray
Some may be forced but it's my choice to wait for good clay
Since working with quality can make the difficult feel like play
For happiness and peace there's no exchange worth time or praise

Seen & Gleaned

When I was a child I started noticing how people can be
I saw the sweetest give sweets and the meanest be mean
I heard stories from kids about being beat while they dreamed
By parents who acted like they were all meek and heavenly

I knew people who others thought were quiet or honest
But they were people I knew to be nothing near that fact
Even those others said were faithful and have their back
I knew to be those who run away like frightened bunnies

You have likely seen similar contradictions to things professed
People saying they are all about reaching out and helping others
But don't or won't even with the help of you and your cousins
Still you hoped no matter what that person gave his or her best

I so strongly contend response-able individuals are rare
Maybe you've gleaned I've seen a lot and am untrusting
This negates not that the true self is what all must bring
Analyze faces people show and accept them if you dare

Knowing how a person can be is knowing their humanity
Learning not to rely on opinions is learning to live off evidence
Being a person that thrives off whims is to be one of circumstance
One applying errors seen is applying wisdom gleaned earnestly

Value Variance

Quality matters with each acquisition
Bounty determines possibility of retention
Material composition and treatment remains core
History of the item matters more now than before
Aesthetics are a given and tip no scale
Hues of all shades for me work well
Textures and patterns are the make or break
Opinions of others skip like rocks across a lake
Each has a preference that may not match mine
Knowing my desires minimizes selection time
Scant options fail to propel me to desperation
Labels for limited use are only worth separation

Gratuities

People accept tips from the north, south, east and west
We all can use a tad extra and cash most times is best
Why not thank good work with a few extra bucks
Or offer sincere words to lift someone in need up
Even visiting nursing homes is a great way to contribute
Just as coordinating a job fair for veterans is a good salute
You don't need a lot of money or time to get involved
Numerous are ways to show thanks or see problems solved
Committing to yourself always flows over to your community
Thank God for your life by showing appreciation and unity

Freedlings One

Constantly bowing as it swims; the swan greets, thanks, honors
Saying hello and good-bye, wishing all wellness as it floats past

***

While time is short and bosses retort the lazy worker does best
Xenophiles screaming dashing like lightening find their rest
Also stress and the heart attack people get chasing that check
Zealous cryptkeepers' corporate reapers true test and regress
But rich and poor are totally pleased receiving these nonetheless

***

I seldom give me the chance to express the depth of my grief
I am who suppresses wells because to me my tears are rocky
Not the balance representative of my taste so I exterminate them
Killing them but remembering the cause to avoid any repetition

***

Saying hey man, ah mister, or yo kin
In a room or on a sidewalk full of men
Never gets the attention of only the one you had in mind
Going dear God, my god, or any god puts you in the same bind
Psalms of David and other scriptures use many names
Reasonably that's why no one can place condemning blame
About others not knowing other daily truths
Instead preferring to congregate with the weekly group
Sing praises unto my name Jah is what is written
Evidence is rare that this scripture is applied or bitten

Tuckered Innocence

Tired of being open
Tired of waiting
Tired of taking tokes off time
Tired of anticipating
Tired of hearing empty words
Tired of having sentiments
Tired of the limbo of loves
Tired of being innocent

Earnest Await

I've been waiting so long for you
That waiting is not an option
Rather is only an unconscious
Motor function opting to control
My joy, my hope, my future
My fortunate way of coping
With the days and years of delay
And denial while being constantly
On trial for nothing other than
Being me, and being then and now

A Nuclear Evolution

During the time the life develops and exits
Bests be received are wanted by and for
Hopes of goodness and ease abound
As breaths are grabbed and cries herald

She is just as sad as she is happy
She is as worried as she is faithful
He is as detached as he is connected
He is just as concerned as he is sure

The life gains and becomes grown
Soon it moves to disembark to live
She realizes and he readily accepts
She keeps care as nothing has changed

She says she can't help but hold on
She says she prays for its protection
She says she knows God will keep life
Yet she still gives in when fear weighs

She finds it hard to trust life will survive
He knows the dependency it has on her
He sees the struggles and wants to aid
She keeps reaching even when shut out

Her nurturing direction and his supportive hand
Keep members grounded through choices good and bad
Whether in one home or seven and getting along or not
The unit remains and is unchanged by past or demise

Strokes, Lines & Brushes
(A First Exhibition)

Dotted, solid, dashes
Lay, run, cross and blend

Atop soft backgrounds and canvass ends
Edging past chunks of clay and faces of men

Feathered with messages
To live and lend
Liberally to all
Breathing deep of Earth's wind

As they gaze upon portraits or abstract bends
Even blurring eyes to see what was worked to send

Placing stock in the lot
And reinvesting the dividends

With splashes of colors for every hallway or den
Ideal as a gift to self, a relative, love or friend

Food gobbled, drinks gulped
Rooms fill with chats and grins

Good painting, bad painting, the curators state and defend
Priced right, a few sold tonight, whose turn is it to bartend

Uniform Differences

Although they are distinct, the differences are similar
They all say they're unique, instead they're being identical
A sunflower is not a violet, still both are types of flowers
A person is not property, each able to offer protection and power

Visual Basics

It is futile
To be in denial
About what you clearly see
Whether water or coffee
Something is needed
To wake you, child
Rise up immediately

Zoo Animals

Elephants, donkeys, hyenas, snakes, and turkeys
Gathered the lions, cheetahs, wolves, hawks and zebras
To end the day with a truce by feasting on those Bush left behind

Questionable Responses

Avoiding questions should be done before they're thought or posed
Interrogations are aggressive questions enabling cases to be closed
Taking long to answer under pressure or tangoing with your words
Can have you swimming with fish or getting dressed with jailbirds

Whistling Rock

In the valley of the mountains
In the wide-open terrain
Sits a rock that whistles
Lumped unmovable on the desert sand
Cacti and wild grass grew to encircle and shade
The contributor to the music
The running wolf made
Before briefly pausing with a paw rested
On the perfectly perched chunk
Just as the water rippled
From the gnat that lit in the oasis
Before the people approached
As breezes blew crescendos
And bounced over peyote
And between prickly green tridents
Past the mock tomatoes
To limbo longer with its trio
While the wolf resumed its run
Leaving sand grains dancing
To the melody carried in the wind
In sync with the ground's percussion
Steady pulsing the rhythms
Belted by the whistling rock
Saluting the setting sun

Armored Partners

I don't know who's more protected
I hope it's me but I wonder whose is the thickest
My gear or that of my armored partner
Between us two, we think he takes his off the quickest

A wall, a window
Good for décor and defense
A nook, a curtain
Good for an impromptu trench

A little rust on the gate
Good warning about the uninvited
A quick wave when to and fro
Good way to avoid what's not delighted in

Good times with good feelings
A moment we can commit to full throttle
Good love and supportive backing
A fulfillment too sizeable for bottles

Good decisions mean good futures
A belief we both hold and enact
Good people make good company
A peace at home we keep intact

I wasn't told who said it but was told the grim prediction
We laughed until cramped from jokes the outsiders barter
Crediting their effort to idle gossip that lacks erudition
Over time they will see we are impenetrable, armored partners

Cottony Curls

As kinky as possible
As straight as can be
As black as genetically able
As healthy as green tea

My hair is soft with a natural sheen that captures eyes
The intrigued want to touch while rollers just despise
What society calls nappy-headed or Queen Apartheid
Is a proud creation fearless of rain or convertible rides

European by taint way back down the line
Choctaw by tribe and traditions, DNA tests still pending
But identifiably and thankfully African by design
So Black or Negro is my claim, else would be pretending

My afro when short stands and when longer lays
My twists unraveled add texture to the locks the wind command
My braided extensions down to my butt I also give an “A”
My freshly-washed, still-wet natural too is loved by my man

As we enjoy the rainy spring and sweat through our hot summer
We adventure to park each other past skies above the world
Laughing and chatting it up until libido makes us dumber
He gently kisses and strongly strokes while gripping cottony curls

Newly Opportune

When the challenge was presented and weighted
I knew it to be possible with sacrifice and risk
Sacrifice of time and risk of scrutiny
But how can I say I was given an opportunity
If I choose to deny the moment to achieve an objective
I'm not allowing for myself a full measure
Of capability to gauge aptitude or ineptitude
The most interesting possibilities
Are the unfilled, not attempted, or newly opportune
Those that before this moment may not have been
Convenient to try, or a reasonably bearable sacrifice
But now is. There is always room for some things
Accommodations are often made for the yet-to experience
And frequently made for the good-before experience
Regardless of how inopportune a scheduled or sudden task
Or how ignorant of the new subject the responder may be
The opportunity to legally fulfill dreams
Or do something better or new
Without causing harm to anyone or anything
Deserves to be researched and tried with expediency
For those freedom-focused individuals of improvement
To whom common social scenes qualify for little share of time
And purpose-filled endeavors always prove newly opportune
Those that before this moment didn't or couldn't fit
But now can be worked out, scheduled and handled

Freedlings Two

As a real friend, I have to say you have totally let yourself just go
And put on the habits and mindset of someone going with the flow
When flying high you can't tell when the wind will cease to blow
So I hope you have a parachute since planes get crashes not tows

***

Appreciating an artist's offerings
Extends past purchases
It begins with your interest then contact
Includes your event appearance(s)
And encompasses your referral
Of friends, family and strangers
Survival means conquering nasty rumors
Or negative comments about works called weird
Yet it's been mostly through death
That the starving and celebrity are wholly embraced
Lovingly heartfelt are the compliments and defenses
Once the artist can give no more for free or pay
Some look and wonder if that existed before the last day

***

Everyone seems to be too busy for this or that
Sometimes too busy for business heads and family chats
But everyone has the flexibility to fit in what they want
And a right to prioritize and choose to do a thing or don't

Duties Of Daredevils

Coasting like kites
Jetting mid-air for hourly seconds
Crashing through red timbers on fire
Ringing sirens for those who beckon
Coordinated apparel
With a truck, car or bike to match
Faithfully trained for safe entertainment
And earning the purse de jour for his favorite catch

Honey Butter

For no material thing will I trade
My biscuit baby spread with marmalade
Whipped honey butter on a toasted delight
Served every time with all its might
Sure you'd like a sample but I sanction none
Honey the butter will have you talking singsong

Manhattan, Chicago and Jackson

I've always wanted to live in Manhattan.
I've always wanted to visit Chicago.
I've always wanted to die in Jackson. My family lives in Jackson.
I enjoy being a well-connected visitor in Manhattan.
I enjoy being occupied in Chicago and nursed in Jackson.
I order the drink sharing the name when longing for Manhattan.
I always fly there and to Chicago. I usually drive to Jackson.

Euphemism & Hyperbole

Diplomacy requires consideration and truth
Yet many allow the occasion to alter dictates
Reputations of all should be handled the same way
Despite the program being a funeral or wake

But some speakers choose to tell more or less
Adding to and taking from for the sake of effect
Readily overstating and exaggerating
Assuming everyone grieving elected truth to neglect

Others believe the proper eulogy
Softens all expressions and omits what is willed
Which is anything accurate that may be offensive
So truth is replaced for nice words to dispense like pills

Isn't being a person of integrity
Being a person who is honest and trustworthy
Why shouldn't credibility matter at all times
The living know the past deeds, clean and dirty

We can speak about the good of a life
And stay away from the topics that aren't pretty
Instead of standing or sitting and telling lies
Then chugging out of guilt, going from sad to giddy

Injustices Of A Glorified King

Hate crimes that go unpunished are abuses with sanctions
He's the man among men and the prize among wives
Human blood is his pleasure when opposition is the prey
His smile lights day and his gate seems a righteous sway

Such as his people sing, write, record, broadcast, and preach it
And even campaign for leaders to coax instructors to teach it

Scorched skulls swinging from metal poles and trees
Vivacious villages violated by villains earning no victory
He sees cause for celebration and basks in the cut lives
Paralyzed by overwhelming pride as he's fed raisins and plantain

Not knowing the great slaughter was his positioning on the cliff
For with the rise of morning his life will have left his body stiff

Believe In Worry

I think it was Joshua
Who told you to take your stand
Saying choose this day who you'll serve
But he and his household will serve God
The Bible is a book of stories on faith
Written to help families keep focus
Compiled to help cultures keep order
Preached by men, women and children
Who teach messages about God's power
So why are so many believers of today
Consumed with worry instead of faith
Situations can become extremely difficult at times
And some things are said to be easier to say than do
Is it that there are some concerns thought unworthy of miracles
Or is it that more reassurance is needed
To calm or erase the bad thoughts that come to mind
Regardless of a person's religious upbringing or commitment
Wouldn't even an overall belief in a greater good
Override a possible or past negative experience
And if a person chooses to faithfully believe in God
He or she should effort to never
Or at worst to seldom give power to fear
By living as one who chooses to walk tall
In their comfort to believe in worry

Freedlings Three

Keeping your word is what I hoped for
Keeping my silence is your sweet dream
Keeping us together is not worth working for
Keeping you here is suffering ants in the inseam

***

Educators are supposed to do their best when they teach
Parents are supposed to help with homework or get tutors
Doctors are supposed to diagnose and best treat
Parents are supposed to try to shape leaders not looters
Officials are supposed to enforce all applicable laws
Parents are supposed to apply rewards and punishments
Youths are supposed to watch their mouths and paws
Adults are supposed to be exemplary and set the precedent

***

What is the source
Of the hot shot's fire
What is the catalyst
Fueling its speed
A forceful exit
Flammable composition
Only the seen is known
Confident, steadfast, interesting
Downright dangerously
Dealing death

You Gotta Keep It

You say you gotta keep it
Because of how you got it
You gotta keep it

That it took a lot of brainstorming
And heavy debates in crowded joints
To finally get you to this point
It doesn't really affect me
It's totally up to you
You gotta keep it

You say you gotta keep it
Because of where you saw it
You gotta keep it

You gave up a lot of friends
And made a major lifestyle change
Several creations now bear your name
If that's the reason
How can I argue
You gotta keep it

You say you gotta keep it
Because another would want it
You gotta keep it

You let it rot, corrode or cover with dust
Buried in a forgotten box in the closet
Forgiving forgiveness for daily regrets
Utterly ignored and devoid of use
But you say you gotta keep it
You gotta keep it

When The End Comes

This is not an ode
To my inevitable death or a mesh of epic stories
Neither is it a tribute to some mythic quest to appease the clergy
These expressions celebrate participation
In several a cover-the-naked-page orgies
And since that indulgence is done
I opt to now write a special one
A poem that's all about elegies
Welling from the conscious test
Given by and to the boundless goddess
Calloused not by circuses, bias,
Promise or mindless thesis
Cautious of terseness and God-kids not living their divine best
A timeless waitress working without rest
Was slacking on healing by choosing to sleep less
It is for the health of your eyes
That some of my books have large fonts
Thin books like this and electronic versions
Promote recycled paper and conserving trees, leaves to trunks
When the objectives were met for this exercise
My head hurt so I rested, very glad I pushed and jumped
Thirty in 30 was achieved early in 25
I only need to patiently await the editor's response
I sought to assure a quality work to help messages avoid jams
Adding personal stories and life tips for readers and poetry fans
I had resolved it had to happen this month or this year, word to fam
I leap happily every year as your pearl is harvested from this clam

Literary & Visual Artists

The Poet & Author

Mylia Tiye Mal Jaza (aka Mary Michelle Jefferson) wrote the poems included in **Elegies Of A Goddess** in October 2009 to capture the history of some of the human experiences she endured directly or witnessed others encountering throughout her lifetime. She is a Mississippi native and Uptown Dallas entrepreneur who has eight other books to her credit to date.

Two of her books were works she republished that were written by ancestors of hers – The Facts Of Reconstruction by John R. Lynch and The Old Negro And The New Negro by T. Leroy Jefferson, M.D. The six books she wrote prior to **Elegies Of A Goddess** ranged in content from original poetry/prose and research to a novella and full-length film and television scripts. Those titles are: Life Is Beautiful: La Vita E Bella, Life Is Beautiful: La Vita Es Hermosa, Seen In Other Words, Plea For Peace, All For Show, and Scientific Evidence God Exists.

A former track-star-turned-model and established journalist / editor for newspapers and magazines, Mary also operates an investment club that holds shares of stocks including Google, Disney, Microsoft and CVS. Additionally, she gives back to the community by cleaning highways, feeding the homeless, and providing school supplies to youth. The businesses she owns provide companies and individuals with assistance that includes human resources, advertising, media relations, technical writing, client servicing / case and project management, and book publishing. *(peoplewarmers.7p.com, bepublished.org)*

The Editor

T. Shani Scott, born in Houston and reared in Dallas, attended Oklahoma City University and is the author of The Rough Side/The Soft Side by Shani Smith – a book exploring a woman's battle to overcome depression.

Shani and her husband, Carl, are the proud parents of four children and serve as mentor to a number of other youth in Dallas and Collin counties through their organization named Christian Youth Sports Association. Through CYSA, they also coordinate and host carnivals and other family events. The couple also operates a screen-printing company.

Shani has successfully performed public relations for professional athletes and other celebrities, and is a former #1 rated radio personality. The Miss Dallas contestant has more than 12 years of radio experience in various markets throughout the country. She has also worked for corporations and daily and weekly newspapers, and coordinated fundraisers and after-school programs for youth. *(christianyouthsports.com, scottygyrl.com)*

The Cover Artist – Version 1

A Chicago native first taken to an art exhibit by her sister (Carrie Jordan, author of ON STAGE: A Collection Of Skits & Plays), Atlanta resident **Deboraa "Goobs" Jordan**'s love for art was solidified after she attended the Picasso showing at the famous Chicago Art Museum and her family supplied her an enormous amount of arts and crafts materials.

She first began drawing shoes and paper doll clothes, and after graduation from Aquinas Dominican high school in Chicago, Deboraa attended Siena Heights University in Adrian, Michigan, on scholarship. An avid traveler, she has visited places including Paris, London, Brussels, Brazil, Australia, Hawaii, Mexico, The Caribbean, Fiji, Barcelona and Madrid.

To date, Goobs has had artwork standing in places including the Hampton Estate and Starbucks Coffee outlets in Dallas and the DFW Metroplex respectively; has donated works to places including Dallas' Black Academy of Arts and Letters; and was an exhibiting artist taking part in Starbuck's "Art of Coffee" campaign as they rolled out a new chilled drink at an Addison, Texas, store.

Her first painting was sold in 1975 for $300, and one of Goobs' pieces was shown during the first Black Expo in Chicago. An excellent visual artist who is well-versed in multiple mediums, Deboraa has received a number of honors and awards from entities including the Gold Blatt's Department Store in Chicago.

It was her initial cover design that inspired Sun Child Wind Spirit's cover design appearing on the second edition of **Elegies Of A Goddess** by Mylia Tiye Mal Jaza.

(artistandfriends.com)

www.ingramcontent.com/pod-product-compliance
Lightning Source LLC
LaVergne TN
LVHW012034160826
845678LV00013B/2591

* 9 7 8 8 6 9 3 4 8 4 5 4 3 *